The Invisible Injury

Delton Myers

This special book belongs to

Dedication Page

This book is dedicated to my grandmother Joyce D. Myers-Rankin. Thank you for believing in me.

DeltonMyers
vi

Lately Peggie the Pig was

feeling very sad and couldn't

understand why.

Last week Tyrone the

Turtle and Brendan

the Bear asked Peggie to come outside

to play kickball.

She sadly said,

"No, thanks."

Peggie stayed in her room all day

feeling down and gloomy.

Tyrone the Turtle was having

a birthday party.

He invited Peggie the Pig to come

to his party.

She sadly said

no again.

Peggie the Pig stayed at home and cried in her room.

Later that week Peggie the Pig's parents took her to the doctor to try to understand why Peggie was feeling so sad.

The doctor diagnosed Peggie the Pig with depression. "Depression is an invisible injury that makes you feel sad," the doctor told her.

Peggie the Pig's parents found Peggie

a special doctor called a child therapist.

A child therapist is someone Peggie

 can talk to about her feelings.

Peggie was able to open up and talk about the sudden passing of her grandma.

Peggie talked about all the fun times she used to have with her grandma.

Now Peggie the Pig meets with her therapist,

Dr. C. Howard, once a week.

When Peggie talks to her therapist,

she feels comfortable and open about

her feelings.

Now Peggie the Pig is feeling better about her feelings and playing with her best friends, Brendan the Bear and Tyrone the Turtle, again.

The End

Acknowledgments

Thank-you to my mom, Deidre Myers-Jeffcoat, and dad, Anthony Jeffcoat, for always trying to make me become a better person today than I was yesterday.

Thank-you to my mentor and teacher Mrs. Tia Geiger. Thank you for your extra push and endless support.

Thank-you to Ms. Raquel M. R. Thomas for making time to help make my dreams come true.

Autobiography

Delton Myers was born and raised in Columbia, South Carolina.

He has a loving elder sister named Demauri and a witty little brother named Brendan Dice, making him the middle child of three.

Delton loves reading, playing his PlayStation 4, and striving for excellence in school.

Delton is also the author of a children's book called The Invisible Injury. His book addresses childhood depression and finding help a healthy way to cope through therapy.